3 4028 09354 5326
HARRIS COUNTY PUBLIC LIBRARY

WITHDRAWN

JPIC Magee
Magee, Wes
Topsy turvy a

9.95
830498

D1463701

Topsy Turvy

Animals

Wes Magee • Tracey Tucker

QEB

A pair of striped zebras
are climbing a tree.
Giraffes on vacation
swim in the sea.

The polar bear cubs try to take off and fly as butterfly snowflakes appear in the sky.

King penguins and reindeer
drive fast cars on ice.
A walrus is writing
a song with brown mice.

A family of lions have baked beans for lunch.
Huge hippos and rhinos play soccer. Crash! Crunch!

Spotty snakes fly like
arrows over the dunes.
Scorpion robbers steal
knives, forks, and spoons.

Gazelles and gorillas
dress up for high tea
and lemurs lick ice cream
while watching TV.

The bald eagle puts
a wig on his head.
Fat yaks paint their faces
green, yellow, and red.

Camels love strumming
guitars in a band.
Look! Line dancing lizards
kick up storms of sand.

Wild bison in sunglasses, high heels, and hats are whirling and twirling with chipmunks and cats.

A goat in a cloak
waves a magical wand.
A gaggle of geese chase
a fox past the pond.

Pink elephants in boots love to stamp and to stomp!
Orange monkeys are paddling their boat in a swamp.

Macaws take a bath
in a crocodile's jaws!

A ladybug laughs
and a dragonfly roars.

Three tigers do somersaults over a wall,
while meerkats on stilts lose their balance...and fall!

A big grizzly bear gets a "Boo!" from a goose.
High up in the hills is a cartwheeling moose.

A heron's conducting
The Frog and Toad Choir.
Dogs do the high jump but
the hamsters leap higher!

A horse and a hare kick-box all day,
while rabbits and rats clean up Santa's sleigh.

Kangaroos win gold
in the hop, skip, and jump.
Koala bears fall
from trees with a bump.

When pandas and panthers
are packed off to school,
those greedy old gibbons
grab seats by the pool.

An emu and ostrich
are so scared of ants,
they only go out wearing
green spotted pants.

Two hens on the roof lay their eggs in hats.
One blue egg rolls off and lands SPLAT on the cat!

Next Steps

Rhymes are a unique way of introducing children to the imaginative potential of stories, word play, and creativity. Coupled with detailed illustrations of a wild and wonderful topsy turvy world, this book provides a springboard for children to explore their imagination and develop their own reading and writing skills.

LISTEN AND LOOK

Take some time to read the book. Look at the illustrations together. Can the children name and point to the animals and what they are doing? Read the book again and see if the children can anticipate and join in with the rhyming words.

WRITE AND RHYME

See if the children can write a simple poem together. It helps if you get them started, perhaps like this...

> The lion is eating.
> The walrus is singing.
> The giraffe is swimming.
> The rabbit is skateboarding.
> and so on...

The use of the "ing" ending in each line gives the poem a rhyme chime, and also some rhythm. How many lines can they complete? The poem can end with a join-in chorus:

What
a
lot
of
animals!

Ask the children to perform their poem aloud. The chorus rises to a crescendo!

RHYME AND IMAGINE

What would a Topsy Turvy world be like for the children? Encourage the children to think about the sequence of their day. What time do they get up? What do they have for breakfast? How do they get to school? Ask the children to think of six things about their day and what would happen if everything turned upside down.

Talk about the children's ideas for a Topsy Turvy world and pick up on different words. For example, "I get up when it's dark", using the word "dark" to create a rhyme list: dark, shark, bark, lark, park, ark, mark, spark, and so on. Can the children create rhyming couplets drawing on the rhyme list to write about *My Topsy Turvy World*? It could begin like this…

> I get up when it's dark.
> I eat breakfast with a shark.
>   In my Topsy Turvy World.
>
> I play football with a lark.
> I hear a robin redbreast bark.
>   In my Topsy Turvy World.

Create further rhyme lists based on words such as "sea", or "band", or "chair". Can the children create more rhyming couplets?

PAINT A PICTURE

This book has some wonderful illustrations. Ask the children to illustrate their poem *My Topsy Turvy World*. The children can separate each verse so there is one per page and then illustrate it to make their own little book. They could even create a front and back cover. Share the book with friends and family.

Learn and Discover

Topsy Turvy Animals features a comical cast of animal characters doing weird and wonderful things. But what do they do in real life? Ask the children to choose their favorite illustrations in the book and discover more about that animal. Find some photographs of animals in the wild and make a collage with facts you have discovered. For example:

- *Tigers* are the largest wild cats in the world. Adults can weigh up to 800 pounds and measure up to 11 feet long! Unlike many other cats, they like water. They are good swimmers and often cool off in pools or streams.

- *Meerkats* are excellent diggers. They like to live in underground warrens in large groups. Meerkats eat plants and fruits as well as lots of insects, such as termites, flies, and butterflies, and even small rodents and reptiles, when they can catch them!

- *King Penguins* are the second largest penguin species. They have four layers of feathers to help keep them warm on the cold islands where they live. While other birds have wings for flying, penguins have flippers to help them swim in the water.

Quarto is the authority on a wide range of topics.

Quarto educates, entertains and enriches the lives of our readers—enthusiasts and lovers of hands-on living.

www.quartoknows.com

Publisher: Maxime Boucknooghe
Editorial Director: Victoria Garrard
Art Director: Miranda Snow
Editor: Sophie Hallam
Designer: Mike Henson

Copyright © QEB Publishing 2016

First published in the United States in 2016 by QEB Publishing, Inc.
6 Orchard
Lake Forest, CA 92630

All rights reserved. No part of this publication may be reproduced, stored in a retrieval system, or transmitted in any form or by any means, electronic, mechanical, photocopying, recording, or otherwise, without the prior permission of the publisher, nor be otherwise circulated in any form of binding or cover other than that in which it is published and without a similar condition being imposed on the subsequent purchaser.

A CIP record for this book is available from the Library of Congress.

ISBN 978 1 60992 998 5

Printed in China

Harris County Public Library
Houston, Texas